Library of Congress Cataloging-in-Publication Data
Burstein, John.
The mind / by Slim Goodbody ; illustrated by Terry Boles.
p.   cm. — (Wonderful you)
Summary: Uses verses, facts, and experiments to introduce the brain and how it works, and explores that quality of the brain known as the mind, which gives us thoughts, feelings, and imagination.
ISBN 1-57749-020-7
1. Brain—Juvenile literature. 2. Thought and thinking—Juvenile literature. [1. Brain. 2. Thought and thinking. 3. Mind and body.] I. Boles, Terry, ill. II. Title. III. Series: Wonderful you (Minneapolis, Minn.)
QP376.B872   1996
612.8′2—dc20   96-9126
                                                                            CIP
                                                                            AC

Cover design by Barry Littmann.

First Printing: September 1996
Printed in the United States of America

00 99 98 97 96   7 6 5 4 3 2 1

Published by Fairview Press, 2450 Riverside Avenue South, Minneapolis, MN 55454.

For a current catalog of Fairview Press titles, please call this toll-free number: 1-800-544-8207

Publisher's Note: Fairview Press publishes books and other materials related to the subjects of family and social issues. Its publications, including *The Mind,* do not necessarily reflect the philosophy of Fairview Hospital and Healthcare Services or their treatment programs.

The paper used in this publication meets the minimum requirements of American National Standard for Information Sciences—Permanence of Paper for Printed Library Materials, ANSI Z329.48-1984.

THE MIND

Slim Goodbody

illustrated by Terry Boles

Fairview Press
Minneapolis

If you didn't have a brain—

You couldn't hear
A choo-choo train.
You couldn't taste
Or smell chow mein.
You couldn't see
Through a windowpane.
You couldn't feel
An ankle sprain.

You couldn't sail
A ship to Spain
To learn if rain
Fell on the plain.
You couldn't ski
The slopes of Maine,
Or take a trip
Down memory lane.

No thoughts or feelings
Would remain,
All your knowledge—
Down the drain,
If your head
Did not contain
Your wonderful
And brilliant brain.

Your brain is probably the busiest place in the world. Night and day it works to keep you alive and healthy. Here are just a few of the things your brain does for you:

• It receives a steady flow of information from your senses about what's going on around you.

• It constantly communicates with every part of your body to know what's going on inside you.

• It collects and sorts all this information, then decides what to do about it.

• It sends out orders to take whatever action is necessary.

• It makes sure these orders are carried out, then decides if any further action is necessary.

Amazing Fact!

✳ At birth, your brain weighed only about one pound, but during your first year it doubled to two pounds! It takes about eighteen years for a brain to reach its final weight of three pounds.

Think About

✳ How is your brain like a computer? How is it different? For example, like your brain, computers can answer math problems and check spelling. Unlike your brain, computers run on programs written by others. Can you think of any other similarities and differences?

Your brain's up on top
Like a king on a throne,
Safe and secure
In a room of its own,
Completely protected
By membranes and bone.

Your brain is soft and spongy. It could be easily damaged by bangs, bumps, and falls if it weren't so well protected. Here's how your brain is kept safe:

1 It's surrounded by skull bones—the dome-shaped *cranium* and the *face bones.*

2 It's wrapped up in three separate protective layers called *membranes.*

3 It's cushioned in a special shock-absorbing fluid that lies between the middle and inner membranes.

Experiment

To see how strong the shape of your skull is

Take an uncooked egg, hold it sideways across your palm, and squeeze as hard as you can. The egg won't crack or break!

Explanation: Your skull has an egg-like shape, which is one of the strongest shapes in nature. If it gets squeezed or receives a blow, the force gets evenly spread around the whole surface. No single spot takes all the pressure, so your skull is harder to crack open if you get hit or take a spill.

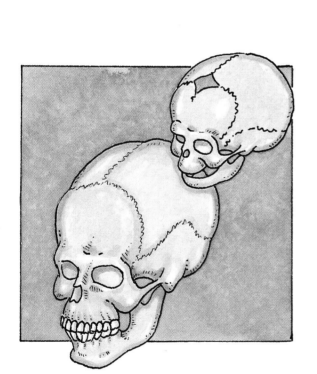

Amazing Fact!

❋ When you were born, your skull bones were soft and slightly separated. This made it easier for your mother to give birth. As you grow up, the bones harden and join together.

Think About

❋ The leader of a country is sometimes called the *head of state.* The command post or control center for an army is called *headquarters.* Why do you think these names are used?

Your Brain's Terrain

Cerebrum

The cerebrum
Is the largest part,
A wrinkly pinkish-gray.
It deals with information
That your senses send its way.

It thinks things through
And then decides
If any action's needed,
And if it is, then to your muscles,
Orders will be speeded.

The cerebrum is divided into two halves called *hemispheres.*

Both hemispheres receive messages from your senses and send out movement orders to your muscles. But each hemisphere has its own special talents.

The left hemisphere is better at language, math, and step-by-step thinking.

The right hemisphere is better at music, art appreciation, and creativity.

Underneath a pinkish covering called the *cerebral cortex,* your cerebrum is white.

Experiment

To use one hemisphere at a time

Sit down and wiggle your left foot for a bit. Put it down and stay still a moment. Then lift your right arm up and move it around.

Explanation: Movement on the right side of your body is controlled by your left hemisphere. Movement on the left side is controlled by your right hemisphere. When you limited your movement to one side of your body, you used one hemisphere at a time.

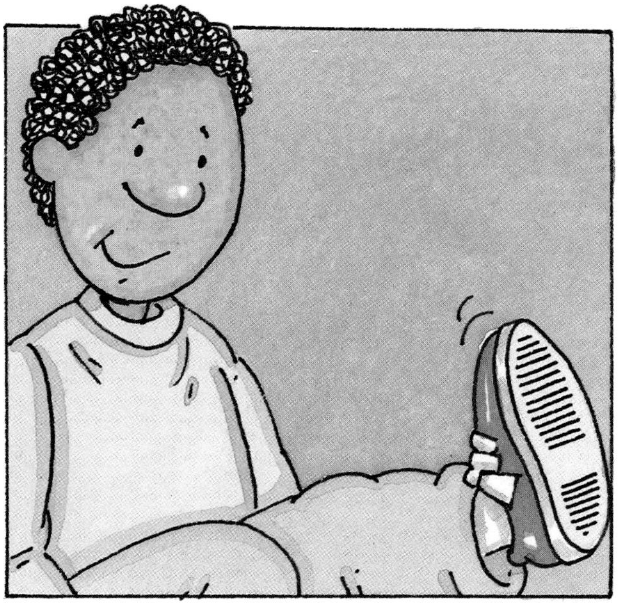

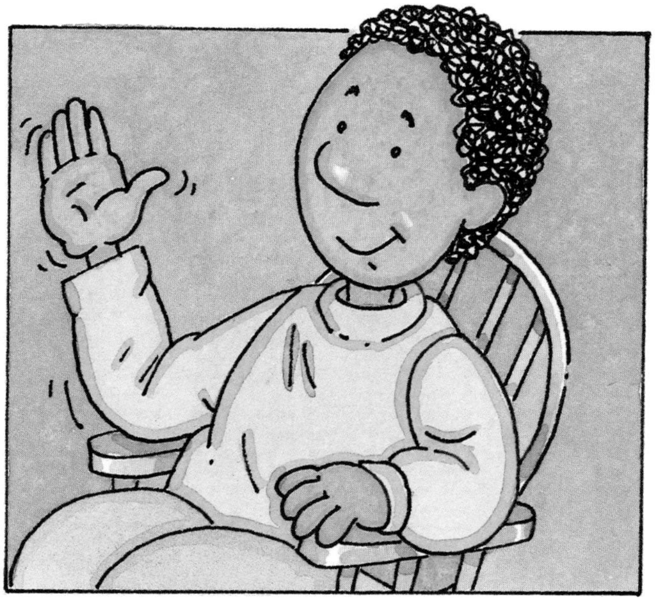

Amazing Facts!

❊ When you have a conversation with someone both hemispheres help out. Your left hemisphere listens to the words to understand *what* is being said. The right hemisphere watches the person's facial expressions and listens to the tone of voice to understand *how* it is being said.

❊ *Cortex* is the Latin word for *bark,* like the bark of a tree.

❊ Your cerebrum's two hemispheres are attached to each other by a bridge of about 50 million nerve fibers! This allows them to communicate and work together.

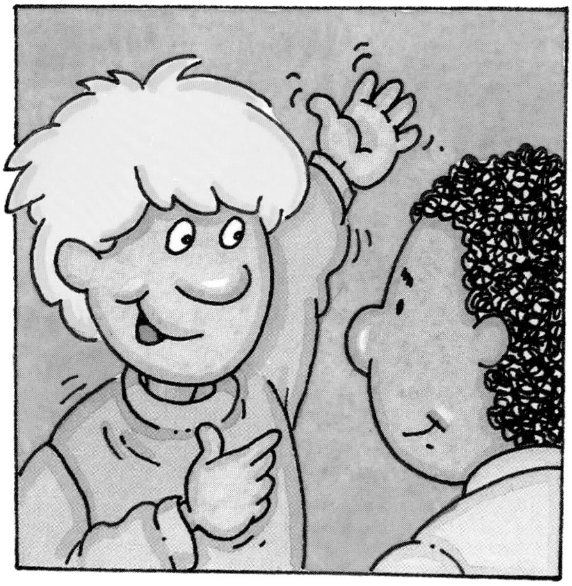

Your Brain's Terrain

Cerebellum

Your muscles get some special guidance
From your cerebellum.
"Work together, nice and smoothly,"
That's what it will tell 'em.

Cerebellum

Your cerebellum is in charge of muscle coordination. That means making sure that the right muscles make the right moves at the right time. With good coordination you seem to do things easily and "automatically."

You may not realize it, but lots of everyday activities take coordination—like walking, for example. You do it automatically now, but when you were a toddler taking your first steps, your muscles didn't work together very well and you fell down time after time. It took a lot of practice before you developed enough coordination to walk with ease and confidence.

Experiment

To understand more about coordination

Take a pencil and write your name very lightly on a sheet of paper.

Explanation: This simple act took a tremendous amount of coordination. You used muscles in your hand, arm, and shoulder. You had to reach out to the right place to pick up the pencil, grasp it, and arrange it between your fingers at the correct angle. Then you had to hold the tip to the paper and move it with enough pressure to write, but not enough to snap the point.

Amazing Facts!

❋ Your cerebellum helps you keep your balance. It receives messages from your inner ear that let it know if you're standing upright or tilting at an angle.

❋ *Cerebellum* is a Latin word meaning *little cerebrum.* The cerebellum is only about the size of your fist—about 1/8th the size of the cerebrum.

Think About

❋ What would life be like without your cerebellum's ability to coordinate muscle movement? What would it be like to try to brush your teeth, tie your shoelaces, or button a shirt?

Your Brain's Terrain

Brain Stem

Controlling what's happening
Under your skin,
Paying attention
To what lies within,

Your breathing and blood flow,
Your temperature, too—
That's what your brain stem
Is doing for you.

While your cerebrum is busy thinking and your cerebellum is controlling movement,
your brain stem is checking on what's going on inside you.

1 One part connects the cerebrum to the spinal cord.

2 Another part controls things such as the speed at which your heart beats and the number of times you breathe in and out each minute.

3 Another part serves as a major relay station—sending messages from your senses to your cerebrum about what's going on in the outside world.

4 One part helps control your body temperature, appetite, thirst, wakefulness, and sleepiness.

Experiment

To prove your brain stem works without you having to think about it

Put your hand over your heart and count how many times it beats in one minute. (Use a clock or a watch with a second-hand). Now jog in place for two minutes and then count again. What changed?

Did you decide to make this change, or did it happen by itself?

Explanation: Your brain stem works without you having to think about it. It always checks on your body's inner conditions. If you need more energy because you're more active, it will direct your heart to beat faster to carry more food and oxygen to your cells.

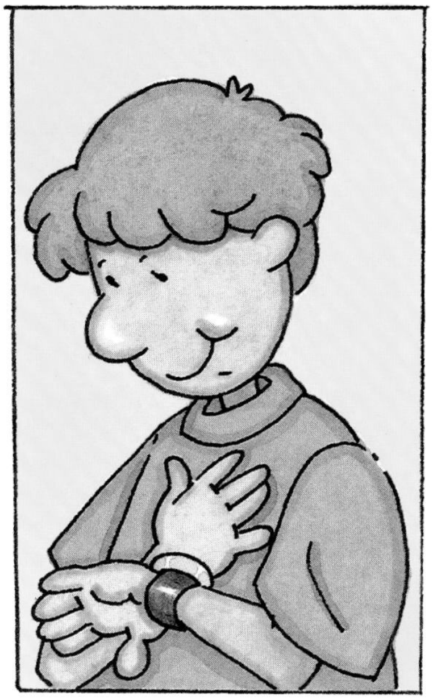

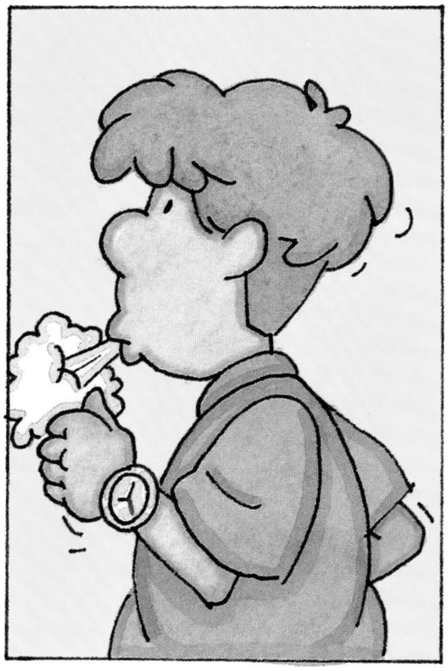

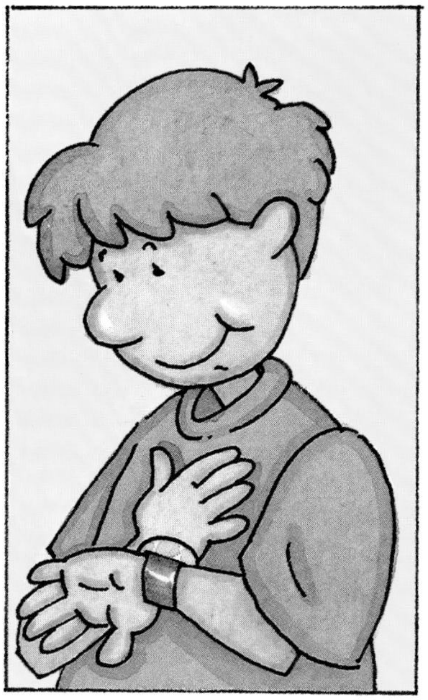

Amazing Fact!

❋ Every second, about 100 million messages bombard your brain from your senses. Your brain stem acts as a filter, allowing only a few to pass through to your cerebrum. Otherwise you'd be so overloaded with information you couldn't figure out what was important and what wasn't, and you'd never get anything done.

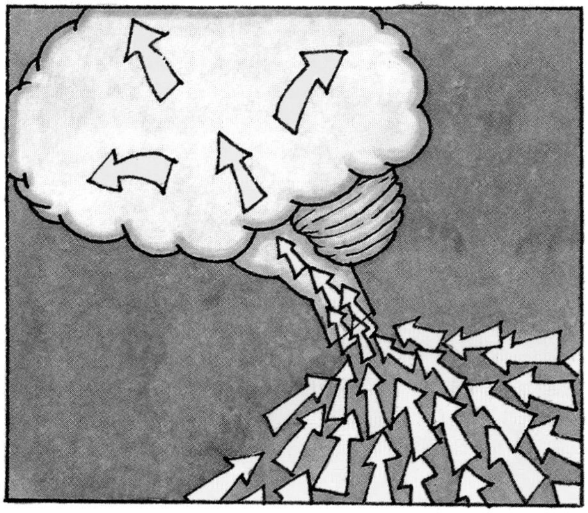

Your Brain's Terrain

Limbic System

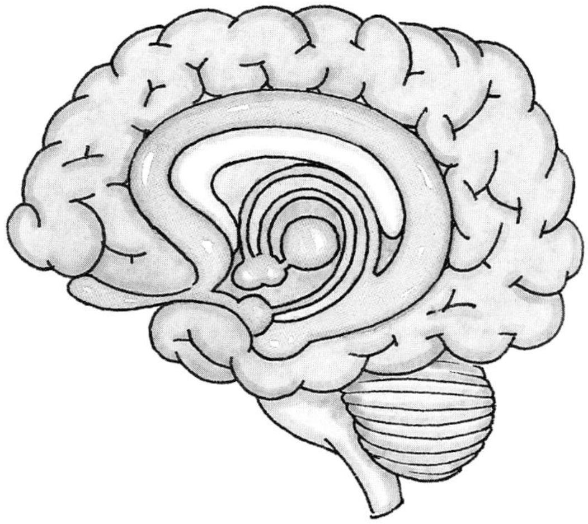

You have so many feelings
It's really hard to list 'em.
Some can be so powerful
You can't seem to resist 'em.
Others are much weaker—
When they pass, you've barely missed 'em.
But all of them are regulated
By your limbic system.

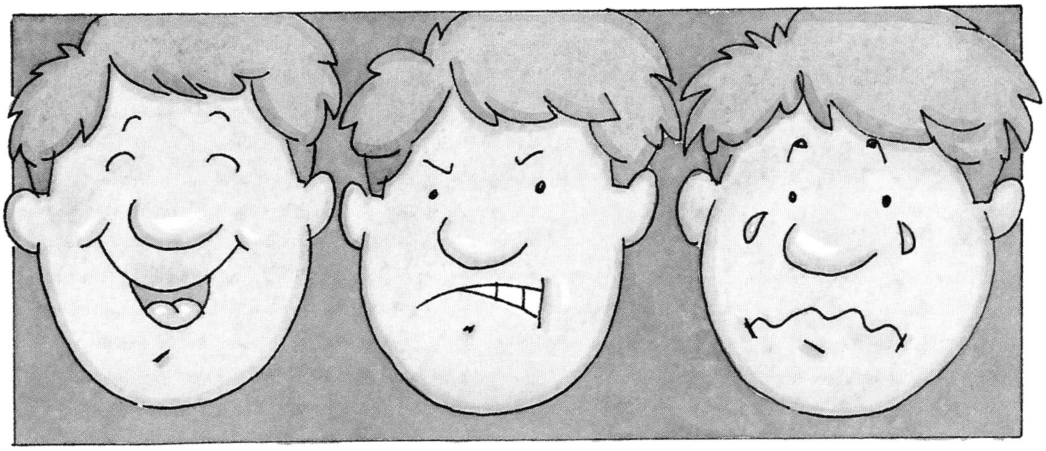

Your limbic system is a special part of your brain that folds around the brain stem. It's the center for your emotions.

Amazing Facts!

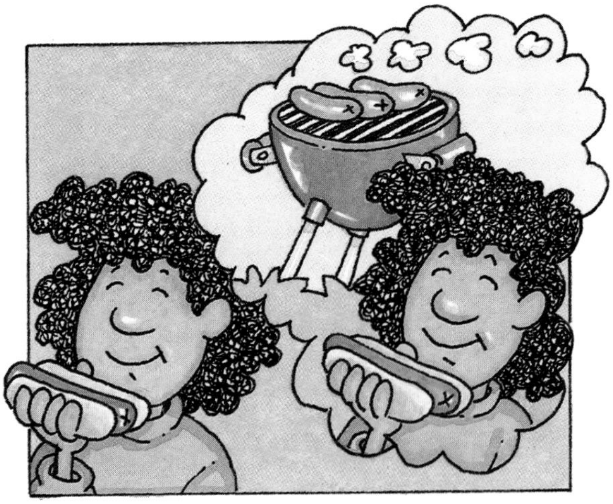

❊ Smell is the sense most directly connected to the limbic system, so a familiar odor can stir strong memories even more easily than seeing a familiar sight.

❊ Because emotions play an important part in our memories, the limbic system helps select the experiences we decide to remember.

Your Brain's Terrain

Brain Cells

Neurons are cells
That make up your brain,
Billions and billions,
And each will contain
Special nerve fibers
That link up to pass
Data along
As quick as a flash.

Messages are sent from one neuron to another, each time jumping across a tiny gap called a *synapse*. Each neuron has three parts:

1 Cell body—to help keep the cell alive.

2 Axons—long fibers that carry messages from one neuron to another.

3 Dendrites—short fibers that receive the messages.

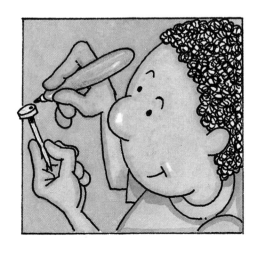

Experiment

To discover the size of a neuron

Find a nail and a fine-tipped black marker. Count how many dots you can make on the head of the nail.

Explanation: Neurons are so small that more than 50,000 of them could fit on the head of a nail!

If somebody died
And their brain was dissected,
And under a microscope
It was inspected,
With all facts about it
Completely collected,
Nothing left out,
Nothing neglected,

There'd be something missing
That couldn't be detected.
The mysterious something
No one would find
Is the wonderful quality
Known as—the mind.

Your thoughts, feelings, dreams, imaginings—all the things that your brain does—that's your mind. If your brain was an instrument, your mind would be the music.

Amazing Fact!

❋ Most scientists believe people only use a very small part—between 10% and 15%—of their mind's true power. That's like using only ten cents out of a dollar.

Around the world
Your mind can race.
It can journey through time
Or tour outer space.
Meanwhile, your brain

Is held firmly in place,
Never departing
Its cranial case,
Safe and secure
In a bony embrace.

Your mind's abilities are almost unlimited. Memories can take you back in time, imagination can take you into the future, curiosity can lead you to a land of new discoveries, and creativity can give birth to wonderful inventions and art. These are just a few of your incredible *powers of mind.*

Think About

❉ When you're lying safely in bed at night—brain in your head and head on your pillow—where are some of the places your mind travels to? How about in school? Can your mind carry you into a world of letters or numbers?

Consciousness

Your mind has a flair
For being aware,
And one of the ways that you show it
Is knowing a fact
And not only that
But actually knowing you know it!

Consciousness is the power of mind that means being aware—and being aware that you're aware! It's one of the most important powers of mind because without it you wouldn't know you knew anything.

You can't be conscious of everything around you all at once. There's just too much. Try thinking of consciousness as a kind of a flashlight you might use in a dark room. There may be hundreds of things all around, but the light only reveals a few of them at a time. Those items are what you're conscious of.

Amazing Fact!

✻ Today alone, you'll probably be conscious of thousands and thousands of different things.

Concentration

Your mind can leap from
Thought to thought,
Hither, thither, and yon.
Ideas fly by and spend a moment,
Then they're suddenly gone.

But sometimes you must pay attention,
Cease this constant exploration,
Rest your mind in one location,
And that's achieved through concentration.

Concentration is the power of mind that allows you to turn your conscious awareness to one idea or subject at a time and focus on it. You use your power of concentration when you study, memorize, take a test, learn important facts, or develop a new skill.

Experiment

To understand how concentration can deepen your understanding

Pick out something to look at—a tree, fruit, plant, or flower—and really concentrate on seeing everything there is to see. Use your senses of sight, touch, smell, and even taste. Are there things you didn't notice at first?

Explanation: By concentrating, you've given yourself the chance to gather a lot more information than you would have if you didn't really focus.

Amazing Fact!

✿ When you get tired, your mind has a harder time concentrating on something. And there are different times during the day when your ability to concentrate is stronger.

Think About

✿ What would happen if you didn't have the ability to concentrate? You couldn't stay focused long enough to even read one page of a book or have a talk with a friend. Can you think of anything else that requires concentration?

Memory

Think how strange your life would be
If you didn't have a memory.
You wouldn't recognize your mother,
You couldn't be sure if you had a brother.
You wouldn't know how to spell your name
Or the rules to play your favorite game.
And any friend you made today—
Why, you'd forget them right away.
The past would simply disappear,
Yesterday and all last year,
January through December,
Erased—because you couldn't remember.

Amazing Fact!

❋ Some people have the ability to look at something just once and remember it in complete detail. For example, they could read this book once and remember it word for word. This ability is sometimes called a *photographic memory.*

21

You have two different kinds of memory:

Short-term memory—lets you hold a small amount of information, like a telephone number, in your mind for a short time. And unless you make an effort to remember, the information vanishes in less than a minute. That's because older items are erased as new ones are added.

Long-term memory—lets you remember things permanently (or at least for a long, long time). It allows you to recall an astounding amount and incredible variety of information—from nursery rhymes to soccer rules.

You develop long-term memory when:

• something happens that involves a lot of emotion, like getting your first bike or going to school for the first time. When feelings are strong, they help you remember.

• you do something over and over again, like repeating a phone number to yourself until it sticks.

Think About

❋ Do you think that by remembering the past, it helps you prepare for the future?

❋ Some things you don't remember at all—like the color of your friend's socks. Why do you think that's so?

Curiosity

Have you ever wondered why
You sometimes wonder why?
And through your mind a million
Different questions seem to fly?

You search and search for answers
'Cause you need to satisfy
Your natural curiosity—
Which makes you wonder why.

Curiosity is the power of mind that leads you to ask questions. The desire for answers—to know how something works or why something happens—is one of the most important reasons that people keep learning and growing wiser.

Amazing Fact!

❇ Thousands of books are printed every year that would never have been written if people weren't curious. What are they? Mystery novels!

Think About

❇ What makes you the most curious? When you have questions, where do you go for answers?

Imagination

You can imagine
A million things—
A cat who talks,
A snail who sings,
A giraffe who flies
On butterfly wings,

Bright fairy queens
And strong lion kings.
Imagination is the power
Helping you achieve
All those happy hours spent
In playing make-believe.

Imagination is the power of mind that allows you to come up with fantastic and amazing ideas—things that may not be real, or even possible, but sure are fun to think about!

Think About

❋ Characters you've seen in movies or read about in books are usually imaginary. But they can still mean a lot to you. Have any of them made you laugh or cry? Have any of them taught you something?

❋ You can use your imagination right now. Imagine a space ship landing and two alien creatures getting off. What would they look like? Can you use your imagination to make them appear stranger and stranger?

Creativity

You know creativity
Is flowing through you
When you snatch an idea
Out of the blue
And use it to make
Something brand new.
You might paint a picture,

Or model in clay,
Make up a dance,
Write a song or a play.
Invent a new gizmo
That whirls and grates—
There's no end to things
That your mind can create.

Creativity is the power of mind that is very closely linked to imagination. But imagination usually involves thinking up ideas in your head, while creativity involves making or doing something in the world.

Amazing Fact!

❋ Creativity has been a natural part of human minds from earliest times. Scientists have discovered cave drawings showing that even our prehistoric ancestors expressed themselves creatively.

Learning

There's always something interesting
And always something new
To keep you learning
Your whole life through.
You learn from grown-ups,
You learn from friends,

You learn in school
That learning never ends.
And besides getting smarter,
There's another reward—
When you keep on learning,
You don't get bored.

Learning is natural. Your mind is like a sponge, soaking up information. There are all kinds of ways to gain knowledge:

• You learn from your own experiences.
• You learn from other people's experiences.
• You learn by imitation.

Think About

❋ Do you think that when you're excited about learning, you can learn more easily?

❋ Language is one of the greatest tools you have for learning. How would you gain knowledge without speech or reading?

Feelings

Sometimes you feel happy,
Then something makes you sad.
You cry a bit and throw a fit
And wind up feeling mad.

You're constantly in motion
On an ocean of emotion—
Waves of feelings come and go,
You ride the tide as feelings flow.

Your emotions are very powerful and serve you in all kinds of ways:

• They can help keep you safe. For example, when you feel fear, there may be danger you need to avoid.

• They can help you enjoy life. For example, you feel happy when you play with friends or a new puppy.

Think About

❋ What happens when you feel angry? How do you deal with that feeling? Do you think anybody's happy all the time? Can anger over-power clear thinking and make you may say or do something foolish?

 # Dreaming

Sometimes your dreams will be delightful,
Other times they might be frightful,
Not to mention weird or strange,
And oh, how quickly they can change!
First you're running in slow motion,
Then you're swimming in the ocean.
Poof! The seas have all run dry,
And you're flying through the sky!
No one ever really knows
What they'll dream up when they doze.

The ability to dream is a power of mind that's essential for maintaining good mental health. But dreams are mysterious and no one knows for sure what they mean. Some people believe dreams help you come up with solutions to problems you faced during the day. Other people think that you dream in order to help you remember people or places you haven't seen for a while.

Amazing Facts!

❋ Most people dream in color, even if they only remember black-and-white pictures.

❋ If you sleep for eight hours, you'll have about a dozen dreams. Altogether you dream about 700 hours a year.

Problem Solving

Your mind is often involved
With problems to be solved,
Challenges to meet,

And assignments to complete,
Coming up with good suggestions,
Finding answers to your questions.

Problem solving is a power of mind that helps with all kinds of problems—small ones, like finding a seat on a crowded bus, and large ones, like what to do if you get lost. You solve problems in many ways:

- By concentrating on them, thinking things through, and coming up with answers.
- By using machines like computers.
- By "borrowing the brains" of others, like getting someone to fix a broken bike.
- By not forcing an answer right away, but "sleeping on the problem."

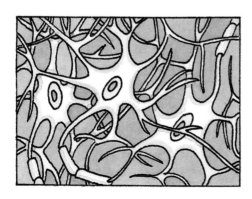

Amazing Fact!

✿ Problem solving involves more of your brain's neurons and uses more of your mind's energy than any other power of mind. It also combines many other powers, like imagination, memory, concentration, and creativity.

Mind and Body Connection

Your mind affects your body
As your body does your mind.
In order to make **one** of you,
These **two** must be combined.

Even though we talk about the mind and the body as if they were completely separate, the truth is that they are closely linked. What you think and feel can change how your body works. What happens to your body can change the way you think and feel.

Amazing Fact!

❋ Some people, by just thinking about it, can speed up or slow down their heartbeat.

Some examples of your mind/body connection are:

• If you imagine something scary happening, your body can start to shake and you might even start to sweat.

• If you feel angry or upset, your stomach can hurt and you may not digest your food very well.

• If your body is in pain, you can't concentrate as well.

• If you feel sad and you put a smile on your face, it can actually cause chemicals to be released in your brain that will make you feel happier.

• If you're upset, you can often calm down by taking several deep, slow breaths.

• If you feel afraid, your heart will beat faster and some of your hairs might stand up on end.

• Exercise can release chemicals in your brain that make you feel happier.

Isn't it wonderful
How you're designed?
You don't change your brain
When you're changing your mind!

Other children's books from Fairview Press

Alligator in the Basement, by Bob Keeshan, TV's Captain Kangaroo
illustrated by Kyle Corkum

Box-Head Boy, by Christine M. Winn with David Walsh, Ph.D.
illustrated by Christine M. Winn

Clover's Secret, by Christine M. Winn with David Walsh, Ph.D.
illustrated by Christine M. Winn

Hurry, Murray, Hurry!, by Bob Keeshan, TV's Captain Kangaroo
illustrated by Chad Peterson

Monster Boy, by Christine M. Winn with David Walsh, Ph.D.
illustrated by Christine M. Winn

My Dad Has HIV, by Earl Alexander, Sheila Rudin, Pam Sejkora
illustrated by Ronnie Walter Shipman

"Wonderful You" Series, by Slim Goodbody
illustrated by Terry Boles
The Body
The Mind
The Spirit